Gastronomic Gatherings

Entertaining with Style

By

Heather A. Allen

MUTTON.

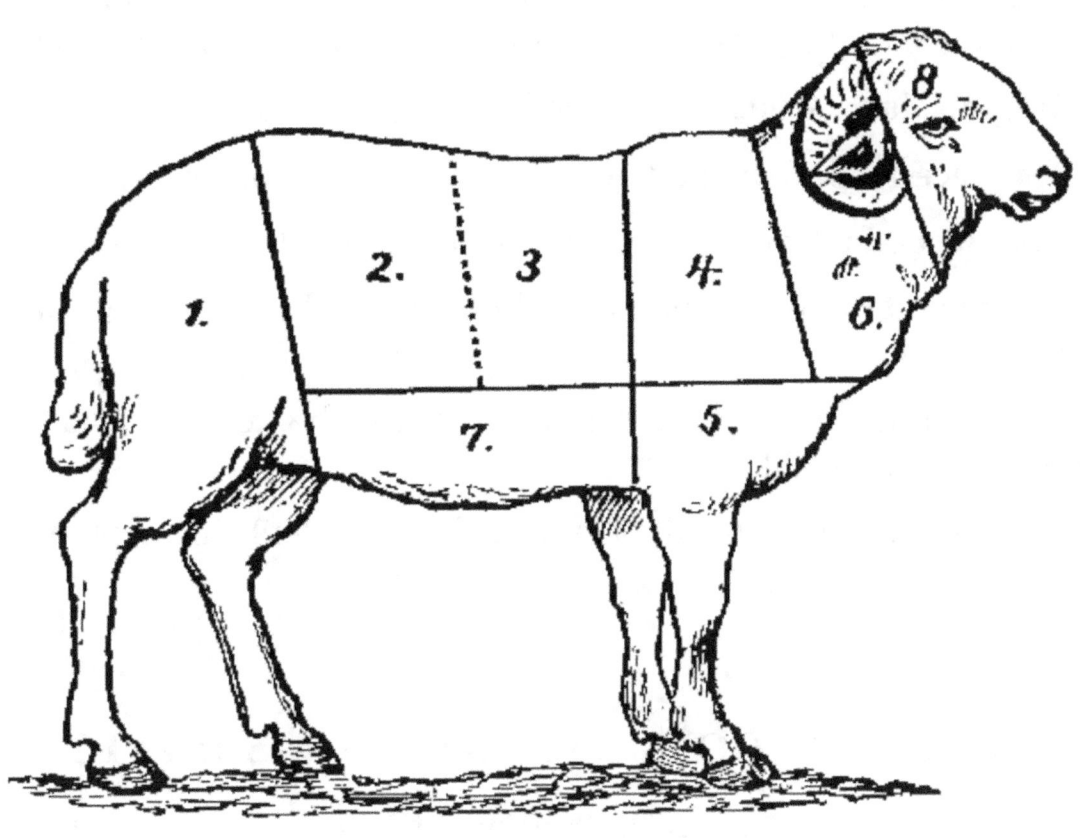

1. Leg
2–3. Loin and small Ribs, or Loin Chops and Rib Chops
4–5. Shoulder and Round Shoulder
6. Neck
7. Breast
8. Head

LAMB OR MUTTON.

Boiled and roasted mutton.

How scraps of mutton may be utilized.

The best time for lambs is from beginning of December to the end of April. Good lamb meat is hard or firm and white and the fat also. Avoid buying soft, reddish meat of lamb or mutton. The forequarter is the most tender part of lamb.

The wether furnishes the best meat when he is 2 to 3 years old. Up to one year it is called lamb meat or lamb, older than that it is called mutton. Good mutton must be juicy, red and covered with a layer of white fat.

Best parts for roasts are leg and loin.

Best pieces for braising and stews are leg, loin and breast.

Small pieces for frying, cutlets and steaks from leg.

Best meat to make bouillon is all lean meat, the feet, scraps of cutlets and bones.

Mutton is less nourishing than beef. It may be kept fresh in vinegar, buttermilk or sweet milk.

Especially old mutton will be more palatable after being kept in vinegar or milk for a while.

No. 1—LEG OF MUTTON, ENGLISH STYLE.

Quantity for 6–8 Persons.

6 lbs. of leg of mutton
Salt
1 pinch of pepper
1 tbsp. of butter
1 small bunch of peppermint
Some vinegar and sugar

Preparation: Remove some fat from the leg of mutton, wash it well, pound it, salt and pepper it, and put into oven with ½ pint of boiling water. Add 1 tablespoonful of butter and roast 1½ hours, basting frequently; the roast will be quite rare inside. If you wish it well done, roast 2 to 2¼ hours.

Wash the peppermint well and chop it very fine, stir it with vinegar and sugar and serve with the meat. If you do not like peppermint sauce, pour off all fat from the roast, add 1½ tablespoonfuls of flour, brown it and pour in 1 cup of water, ¼ cup of cream and let this boil; then season with salt, strain the gravy and serve it with the meat.

No.2—LEGOFMUTT ONINMILK.

Quantity for 6–8 Persons.

6 lbs. of leg of mutton
2–3 qts. of milk
⅛ lb. of bacon for larding
Salt, pepper
2 cloves
½ onion
½ bay-leaf
⅛ lb. of butter
2 tbsps. of flour
½ cup of sweet or sour cream
A few drops of lemon juice
1 cup of water

Preparation: The membrane and fat are removed from the leg of mutton and it is then well pounded and put into sweet milk for 2 or 3 days, turning it twice every day. The milk should cover the roast. In winter leave it in the milk for 3 days, in summer only 2. After this wash it off, lard it, salt and pepper it, put into oven with water, the spices and onion. After roasting it for ½ hour, add the butter, roast for 2 hours, basting frequently.

During the last ½ hour take off some fat, stir in 2 tablespoonfuls of flour and add 1 cup of water, gradually, also the cream and a few drops of lemon juice; now leave it in the oven a little longer. If the gravy has boiled down too much in the last ½ hour, add some more water. The gravy must be smooth and strained before serving with the roast. This is a very good dish.

No.3—LEGOFMUTT ONWITHREDWINE.

Quantity for 6–8 Persons.

6 lbs. of leg of mutton
⅛ lb. of bacon
10 sardines
1 qt. of thin vinegar
2 small onions
3 cloves
10 pepper-corns
⅛ lb. of butter
Salt
1½ tbsps. of flour
½ pt. of red wine
½ pt. of water
1 bay-leaf

Preparation: The leg of mutton is cleared from all membrane and fat, pounded and larded. The sardines are drained and cut lengthwise into halves and the leg of mutton larded with them. The thus prepared leg of mutton is covered with 1 qt. of vinegar, onion slices, cloves, pepper-corns and bay-leaf and left in the vinegar for 24 hours, turning it over once in a while.

After this time the leg of mutton is fried with the butter and after ½ hour the flour is stirred in, add salt and pepper, the ½ pint of water and gradually the red wine. The roast is cooked slowly for 2 or 2½ hours and turned and basted several times until well done. The gravy is strained and served with the roast.

Remarks: If you do not like the taste of sardines, lard with bacon only.

No.4—ROASTEDLEGOFMUTT ONWITH CHAMPIGNONS.

Quantity for 6–8 Persons.

6 lbs. leg of mutton
⅛ lb. of butter
2 tbsps. of flour
2 wine glasses of Madeira
½ pt. champignons
8 pepper-corns
Juice of one lemon
2 cloves
½ bay-leaf
Water or bouillon
Salt

Preparation: The leg of mutton is freed from all fat and membrane, salted and fried in the ⅛ lb. of butter to a nice brown on both sides, and placed on a platter. Brown the flour in the same butter, add ⅛ onion and water or bouillon, salt and spices. Put the meat back into this gravy, it must be half way covered with it, cover it up and roast in oven 2½ hours. Then take meat out again, strain the gravy, take off all fat, pour the gravy back into the roaster, add Madeira and lemon juice, place the meat into it, cover, and cook it ½ hour longer. Finally cut up the champignons and put them into the gravy. Leg of mutton and gravy may be served on the same platter or separately. The gravy must be smooth, not thick.

No.5—STUFFED ROASTED LEG OF MUTTON.

Quantity for 6–8 Persons.

The preparation and contents are the same as No. 4.

The bone is taken out, the cavity is filled with a stuffing as described in No. 11, of the previous chapter, Stuffed Veal Breast, and is cooked just the same as No. 4, of this chapter. You may omit the champignons.

No.6—MUTTON STEW.

Quantity for 8 Persons.

5 lbs. of leg of mutton
½ tbsp. of caraway seeds
Salt
1 large onion sliced
½ carrot
¼ parsley root
Water
A thin white cloth

Preparation: The leg of mutton must be of a good quality. It is pounded, washed and tied into a thin white cloth; then put into boiling water; salt, onion, carrot, parsley root, caraway seeds added and cooked slowly for 2½ hours. The leg of mutton must be white outside and pink inside and juicy. Garnish with parsley and serve. A mustard or caper gravy is served with this meat.

No.7—LARDED SADDLE OF MUTTON, MOCK VENISON.

Quantity for 6 Persons.

6 lbs. of saddle of mutton.
⅛ lb. of butter
⅛ lb. of bacon for larding
½ pt. sweet or sour cream
A few drops of lemon juice
1 tbsp. of flour
Salt, pepper

Preparation: The ribs of the saddle of mutton are chopped off, the outer hard membrane is trimmed off and the bones cut out. Then the meat is pounded and larded, strewn with salt and pepper and put into the pan with the ⅛ lb. of butter with which it is basted very often. Water is added from time to time and cooked one hour. Now the flour is stirred in, ½ cup of water and the cream and lemon juice added and boiled again ½ hour. The meat must be basted very often. The gravy is then strained and served with the meat.

No. 8—SADDLE OF MUTTON A LA ENGLISH STYLE.

Quantity for 6 Persons.

6 lbs. of saddle of mutton
1 pt. of water
Salt, pepper, soup greens

Preparation: The saddle of mutton is pounded and skinned. The ribs are chopped off a little, the fat is left on. Now the meat is salted and peppered and put into the oven with 1 pint of boiling water, and soup greens. Let it roast 1 hour, basting frequently. Then serve.

For the gravy, take 1 tablespoonful of flour, stir it into the drippings and add ¼ cup of cream. Skim the gravy. You can also serve a peppermint sauce as in No. 1. A Bearnaise gravy is nice too.

No. 9—MUTTON TENDERLOIN.

Quantity for 4 Persons.

2 mutton fillets
⅛ lb. of bacon
Salt, pepper
3 tbsps. of butter
½ tbsp. of flour
1 cup of water
Juice of ½ lemon
2 tbsps. of white wine
Bouillon

Preparation: The two fillets are cut from a saddle of mutton, (they are situated below the ribs alongside of the back). Cut the fillets lengthwise and crosswise so they make 8 pieces. Lard each piece nicely with the bacon, salt and pepper it, put the butter into the pan and fry quickly. Then stir in ½ tablespoonful of flour and pour in enough bouillon or water mixed with meat extract so the fillets are almost covered. Cover the pan and cook slowly ½ hour. Finally add the lemon juice and wine. Strain the gravy and pour it on the fillets or serve separately.

No.10—STEWED RACK OF MUTTON.

Quantity for 6 Persons.

4 lbs. rack or rib piece
½ carrot
½ parsley root
½ kohlrabi
½ onion
⅛ celery root
Salt
3 qts. of water

Preparation: The rib bones are partly chopped through and the whole piece of meat bound with string, then boiled slowly in 3 qts. of boiling water, salt and soup greens. When done, put on a hot platter. A mustard or morel gravy is nice with it. The remnant of bouillon is used to cook vegetables in or for soup.

No.11—MUTTON STEW WITH WHITE CABBAGE.

Quantity for 6 Persons.

4 lbs. of lean mutton
1 large head of white cabbage
2 tbsps. of butter
Water
Salt

Preparation: The cabbage is cut into 12 parts and put on the fire with boiling water, then cooked for 10 minutes. The water is then drained off and fresh boiling water put on. The meat is washed and salted, put in and cooked with the cabbage slowly for 2½ hours. Then it is served on a hot platter. The cabbage must not have too much gravy. If it is not rich enough, add more butter. Serve it with the meat and potatoes.

No.12—MUTT ONSTEAK.

Quantity for 6 Persons.

4 lbs. of mutton chops or cutlets
1 piece of butter
Salt, pepper

Preparation: The cutlets are pounded well, and the bones all trimmed out. A pan is larded with some mutton fat and heated. The meat is put in and fried on the stove ¼ hour, turning it over often. Serve on a hot platter, salt and pepper, and butter. A peppermint sauce, as in No. 1, is good with this meat.

No.13—MUTT ONCUTLETSORCHOPS.

Quantity for 6 Persons.

4 lbs. of mutton chops
⅛ lb. of butter
Salt, pepper
½ cup of water

Preparation: The real cutlet piece is the loin with the upper ends of the ribs. Every cutlet must have a rib and be one inch thick. They are pounded, skinned and the fat cut off, salted and peppered. The butter is melted in a pan and the cutlets put in and fried 3 to 5 minutes. Then they are served on a hot platter. For gravy pour some hot water or bouillon into the frying butter and perhaps a little more salt. Pour the gravy over the cutlets and serve hot.

No.14—MUTTON CUTLETS BROILED.

Quantity for 6 Persons.

4 lbs. of mutton chops
1 piece of fresh butter
Salt, pepper

Preparation: The cutlets are pounded and placed on a broiler 5 minutes, turning them once; placed on a hot platter, seasoned with salt and pepper, buttered and served at once.

No.15—BROILED BREADED MUTTON CHOPS.

Quantity for 6 Persons.

4 lbs. mutton chops
Salt, pepper
1 cup grated rolls
3 tbsps. of Parmesan cheese
⅛ lb. of butter

Preparation: Trim off the skin and fat, pound, salt and pepper the cutlets. Heat some butter and dip each cutlet into it, then into a mixture of roll crumbs and Parmesan cheese. Now broil to a light brown on a broiler, which requires 5 minutes. Serve on a hot platter and pour the rest of the melted butter over them.

Remarks: You can also fry the cutlets in a pan; then you need an additional ⅛ lb. of butter.

No. 16—MUTTON CHOPS WITH POTATOES.

Quantity for 6 Persons.

3½ lbs. mutton chops
Salt, pepper
1 pt. cream or milk
⅛ grated onion
2 tbsps. of Parmesan or Swiss cheese
⅛ lb. of butter
2 lbs. boiled, chopped potatoes.
3 yolks of eggs

Preparation: There should be 12 pieces of chops; salt and pepper them and fry them brown on both sides in butter. The boiled potatoes are pressed through a potato masher and mixed well with the remainder of the butter, which is creamed with the yolks of 3 eggs, salt, grated onion, cheese, cream and the rest of the butter which is left in the pan. Half of this mixture is placed into a casserole, the fried cutlets are placed on top and the remainder of the mixture put on to cover them. Then strew bread crumbs over the whole and small pieces of butter and bake in a medium hot oven for ½ to ¾ hour. Serve in the casserole.

No. 17—STEWED MUTTON CUTLETS.

Quantity for 6 Persons.

4 lbs. of mutton cutlets
Salt, pepper
Some bacon for larding
½ pt. of champignons
4 truffles
1 tbsp. of flour
Some bouillon or water mixed with ½ tsp. meat extract
2 tbsps. of butter
1 small wineglassful of Madeira or red wine

Preparation: The cutlets must be 2 inches thick. They are pounded and larded with bacon strips after the skin and fat have been removed from them, then peppered and salted and dipped in flour. Now they are quickly fried in butter and placed on a hot platter.

For the gravy, brown the flour in the butter, add bouillon, wine, salt, and the cutlets. Cover and stew until done. ¼ hour before they are done, skim the fat off and add the sliced champignons and chopped truffles. Serve the cutlets and gravy on the same hot platter. It is best to warm the plates with such a dish.

Remarks: You can prepare the cutlets more simply by omitting the champignons and truffles and putting 4 tomatoes into the gravy. Strain the gravy.

No.18—IRISHSTEW .

MuttonCutletsstewedwithallkindsofvegetablesandPotatoes.

Quantity for 6 Persons.

3 lbs. of mutton chops
1 head of Savoy cabbage
5 kohlrabis
3 small onions
2 lbs. of raw potatoes
Bouillon or water
¼ lb. of butter
Salt, pepper
¼ head white cabbage

Preparation: The vegetables and potatoes are cleaned and peeled well and cut into small pieces. In an iron kettle, which has been buttered, the vegetables are placed in layers, then a layer of cutlets, seasoned with salt and pepper; on this a layer of potatoes and onions; repeat this twice, taking care that you do not season too highly with salt. Potatoes must be the last layer. Fill up with hot bouillon or water. Place a piece of butter on top. Stew or boil for 3 hours, well covered.

No.19—BAKEDMUTT ONKIDNEYS.

Quantity for 6 Persons.

10 mutton kidneys
1 piece of butter
Salt, pepper
½ tbsp. of mustard
Grated rye bread

Preparation: The kidneys are cut half way through, skinned and rubbed with salt and pepper. Melted butter mixed with mustard is put over them and then they are dipped in rye bread crumbs, basted with butter and baked 15 minutes.

This dish is very nice garnished with cooked vegetables.

No.20—MUTT ONKIDNEYPUDDING.

Quantity for 6 Persons.

8 raw mutton kidneys
1 small onion
Salt, white pepper
2 tbsps. of butter
Juice of 1 lemon
1 tbsp. of flour
18 champignons
½ cup of rice
Bouillon or water
1 tbsp. of butter
2 yolks of eggs
½ pt. gravy or broth from the meat

Preparation: The kidneys are sliced ½ inch thick. Butter, onions and sliced champignons are cooked; flour, gravy, salt and pepper are added. The sliced kidneys are put in and cooked slowly 15 minutes. Add lemon juice.

The ½ cup of rice is boiled until soft in bouillon or water to a thick mush, then the butter and finally the 2 yolks of eggs are stirred into it. A pudding mold is buttered and strewn with roll crumbs, then put in a layer of rice and a layer of meat, alternately, until all is in; the last layer should be rice. Cover and cook in a steamer over a kettle of boiling water for 2 hours. After it is done, dump it on a hot platter and serve with Dutch gravy.

No.21—MUTT ONRAGOUT.

Quantity for 6 Persons.

2 lbs. of mutton, lean, without bones
1 large onion
⅛ lb. of butter
Salt, pepper
2 tbsps. of flour
¾ qt. bouillon or water
1 wineglass red wine

Preparation: The meat is cut into 1½ inch pieces. Butter stewed with onion and the pieces of meat are put in to cook 10 minutes. Add the flour and cook another few minutes, then add bouillon or water, salt and pepper and cook until well done. During the last 15 minutes, pour in the red wine and serve with a wreath of boiled rice. (Boil 1 cupful of rice in salt water until tender but retaining its firmness and add a piece of butter).

No.22—MUTT ONWITHPOT ATOES.

Quantity for 6 Persons.

1½ lbs. left over mutton roast
1 onion, sliced
1½ lbs. sliced raw potatoes
Salt, pepper
Left over gravy

1 small piece of butter

Preparation: The meat is cut into small thin slices, also the peeled potatoes. A casserole is buttered and filled with 1 layer of raw potatoes, 1 layer of meat, salt, pepper and sliced onion. Repeat twice, with potatoes for the last layer. Pour the gravy over, (if it is too thick, dilute with cream or milk) put a few small pieces of butter on top, bake in oven for 1½ hours.

If you have no left over gravy, make one of 1 tablespoonful of browned butter, flour, water or bouillon, cream, pepper and salt. Pour over the contents of the casserole and bake it.

No.23—MUTT ONWITHPICKLES.

Quantity for 6 Persons.

1½–2 lbs. of mutton roast or boiled mutton remnants
Scant ⅛ lb. of butter
2 tbsps. of flour
¼ small onion, sliced
1 pt. thin gravy or bouillon
½ tsp. of meat extract
Salt, pepper
1 clove
½ bay-leaf
1 tbsp. of wine vinegar
3 sweet-sour pickles
3 tbsps. of pickled pearl onions
1 tsp. of sugar

Preparation: The cold, fried or boiled mutton is cut into small pieces. The butter and onions are browned, then flour stirred in. Add salt, pepper, cloves, bay-leaf, vinegar, sugar and bouillon or thin gravy and boil until quite thick. The pickles, cut into small cubes, and onions, are now put in, stewed a little while; add the pieces of meat, heat, but do not boil, then serve. If the gravy is too light, add some meat extract or sugar coloring. Fresh boiled, peeled potatoes go well with this dish.

No.24—MUTT ONROASTSALAD.

Quantity for 6 Persons.

1 lb. mutton roast
2 yolks of eggs
Salt, pepper
Some wine vinegar
1 tsp. of mustard
½ pt. cream
4 mustard pickles
1 vinegar pickle
2 tbsps. of pearl onions
2 tbsps. of oil

Preparation: Meat, pickles, onions, all this cut into small pieces and mixed well with the other ingredients, then garnished with hard-boiled eggs.

No.25—MUTT ONPIE.

Quantity for 6 Persons.

3–4 lbs. of mutton from the leg
1 qt. water
⅙ part of a small celery root
2 small onions
Some salt
2½ tbsps. of flour
Juice of one lemon
1 pinch of white pepper
3 doz. oysters
½ pt. can of champignons
2 tbsps. of chopped parsley
2 tbsps. of butter

ThePaste.

½ lb. fresh butter
¼ lb. lard
¾ lb. of flour
2 tbsps. of brandy
1½ glasses water

Preparation: The meat is cut into pieces the size of cutlets, boiled until tender in 1 qt. of water, celery root, 2 small onions, salt. Cook 2 tablespoonfuls of butter and flour and add veal bouillon; then add lemon juice, salt and pepper, if necessary, boil a few minutes, but do not let the gravy get thick.

The Paste: Butter and lard must be very cold. You may omit the lard and use more butter instead if you wish. Both are cut into the flour, the very cold water and brandy poured in and then stirred to a light paste and rolled out on a well-floured board. The butter must be visible all through the paste. Do not knead much. Roll out, line a baking dish with half of the paste, then put in layers of meat, oysters, then sliced champignons, chopped parsley, the gravy poured over the whole and then covered up with the other half of the paste in which make a few cuts, finish off the edge and bake in medium hot oven 1 to 1½ hours.

Remarks: Leave some of the gravy, mix with oyster liquor and the juice of ½ lemon and serve with the pie.

No.26—MUTT ONPIEPREP AREDSIMPL Y.

The preparation of this pie is just the same as in No. 25, but instead of oysters and champignons, take raw, very thinly sliced potatoes.

No.27—LAMBROAST .

Quantity for 6–8 Persons.

6 lbs. of lamb quarter
Salt, pepper

½ lb. of butter
½ pt. sour or sweet cream
2 tbsps. of lemon juice
1 cup of water
1 tbsp. of flour

Preparation: The lamb meat must be two days old. It is pounded, salted, peppered and put into the oven with the cup of water. After 10 minutes the browned butter is poured hot over the meat. Baste frequently, gradually adding the cream and lemon juice, and roast for 1½ to 2 hours.

For the gravy, stir into the butter some flour and a little water and cook (if necessary) a while longer. Serve the gravy with the roast after straining.

No.28—BREADEDLAMBROAST .

Quantity for 6 Persons.

4 lbs. of lamb quarter
Salt, pepper
2 eggs
Finely sifted roll crumbs
1½ cups of sour cream
1 tbsp. of flour
1 tbsp. of lemon juice
1 cup of water
½ lb. of butter

Preparation: The meat is pounded, rubbed with salt and pepper, then rolled in beaten egg and bread crumbs. Heat the butter and fry the meat quickly on top of the stove, then put it into the oven, basting it often and adding the cream in spoonfuls, also a little water, if the butter should get too brown. Cook in slow heat 1½ hours until the roast looks golden yellow; then serve.

For the gravy, stir 1 tablespoonful of flour into the butter, add water, cook and strain. You can also add chopped champignons.

No.29—MUTT ONORLAMBRAGOUT .

Quantity for 6 Persons.

3 lbs. of mutton or lamb
⅛ lb. of butter
Salt
6 pepper-corns
2 cloves
1 bay-leaf
¼ carrot
1½ qts. of water
3 tbsps. of flour
Juice of ½ lemon
1 wineglass red wine
½ pt. can champignons
5 truffles, chopped and peeled
½ tsp. of sugar
½ onion

Preparation: The mutton or lamb, which should be from the breast, is cut into equal sized pieces, stewed a little in 2 tablespoonfuls of butter, then add 1½ qts. of water, carrot, onion, salt, pepper, cloves, bay-leaf and cook the meat until tender.

For the gravy, take the rest of the butter, brown it with flour, add the strained mutton bouillon, the red wine, lemon juice, some of the champignon juice and boil slowly ½ hour. The gravy should be quite thick. Now put in the meat, champignons, truffles and spices and boil 15 minutes longer. Taste it for salt and spices. Serve on a hot platter, and garnish the rim with crescents of puff paste and small fried meat dumplings. The dumplings are prepared the same way as the Ox-tongue Ragout in [No. 35](No. 35), Chapter 2.

No.30—LAMBSTEW .

Quantity for 6–8 Persons.

Head, liver, lungs and heart
Salt
8 whole pepper-corns
1 onion
1 bay-leaf
⅛ lb. of butter
1 egg
Roll crumbs
2 tbsps. of flour
Some herb vinegar
2 cloves

Preparation: The head is split in two, brain and tongue taken out and soaked in water. The tongue is boiled until tender in water with salt, pepper, bay-leaf, cloves and onion. In the same water, cook the brain and also the heart, liver, lungs and head until tender.

When the tongue, heart and lungs are well done, cut them into cubes. All the meat is put into a pot. Season with salt, pepper and a piece of butter, pour in some bouillon and stew. Cut the meat off the head, season with salt and pepper, dip in egg and roll crumbs and fry in butter to a golden yellow. The same is done with the brains. The liver is cut into slices, salted, peppered, dipped in flour and also fried.

The hash of tongue, lung and heart is placed in the middle of a hot platter, the liver slices placed in a wreath around it, the meat from the head, which has been cut into neat pieces, and the brains placed on top of the hash.

The gravy should be prepared before dishing out the hash. For the gravy, take one tablespoonful of flour, stir it in the butter in which the meat, brains and liver have been fried, add some of the bouillon and a little vinegar, lemon juice or white wine. Serve the gravy with the meat.

No.31—PLAIN RAGOUT OF MUTTON OR LAMB.

The preparation is the same as in No. 29. Instead of wine, take wine vinegar or herb vinegar and leave off the champignons and truffles.

PORK.

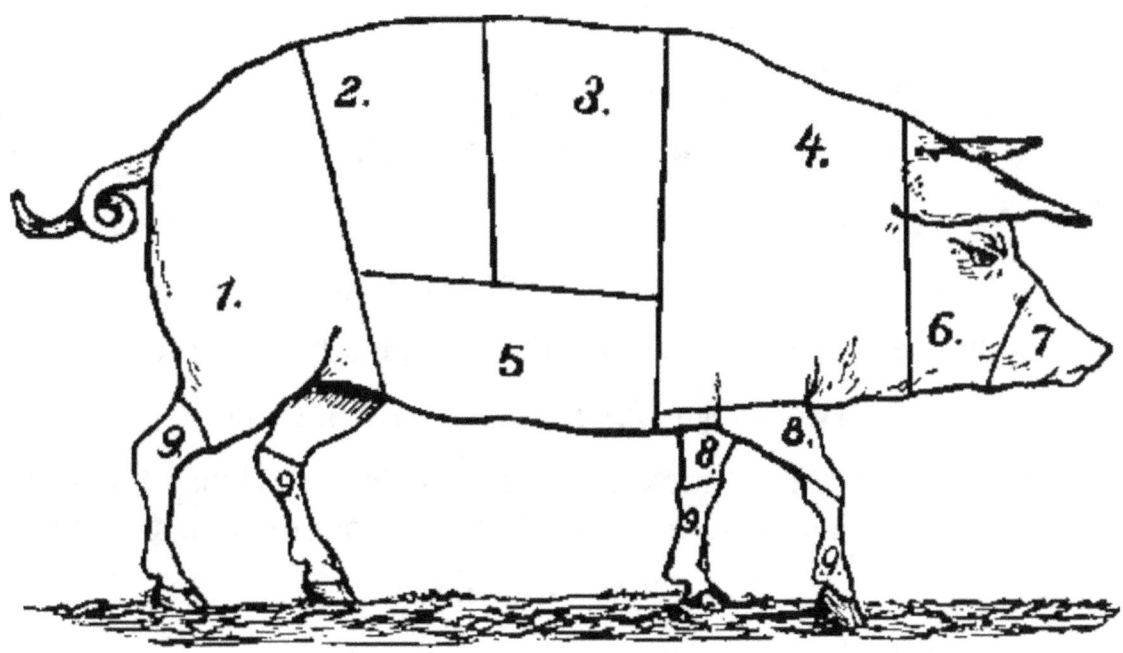

1. Ham.
2. Pork Loin.
3. Pork Chops.
4. Pork Shoulder
5. Belly
6. Head
7. Snout
8. Shanks
9. Feet

Boiled, Fried and Salted Pork.

Also recipes for utilizing left over pork.

Good pork from well fed yearlings is tender, light and not too fat. The fat or lard must be white, the hide light. Inferior pork has a yellow hide, smeary lard and very fat, dark meat.

Suckling pig is considered a delicacy in the kitchen. It is usually 2 or 3 weeks old.

Best Pieces for Roasts.

The leg, the pork loin, the slightly smoked rib piece, the fillets.

Small Pieces for Frying.

The cutlets, the fillets and ham slices.

Best Pieces for Stew.

The pork shoulder and fillets.

Best Pieces for Boiling.

The belly, the hip-bone, (head, shoulder and marbled pieces.

Best Pieces for Smoking and Salting.

The hams, pork loins, smoked tenderloin, (called lachsschinken), the belly for lean bacon, the pork loin as fat bacon, tenderloin and shoulder.

For Gelatines.

The hide or skin and bones.

No. 1—PORK ROAST.

Quantity for 6–8 Persons.

4 lbs. rib roast
Salt
6 pepper-corns
2 cloves.
1 onion
1½ tbsps. of flour
1 cup of cream
1½ cups of water
1 bay-leaf

Preparation: The meat is washed and pounded, some fat trimmed off and salted. The roast is put into the oven with 1 cup of boiling water, all spices and onion and roasted 1½ to 2 hours, basting it frequently. The roast must be crisp outside. When it is done, put it on a platter and prepare the gravy. If there is too much fat, skim it off, put the flour into it, stew a little while, add the cream and some water if necessary, cook, strain and serve with the roast.

No. 2—FRESH YOUNG LEG OF PORK FOR ROAST.

Quantity for 10–15 Persons.

8–10 lbs. of leg of pork
Salt
6 pepper-corns
3 cloves
1 onion
2 tbsps. of flour
1 pt. of water
½ wineglass red wine or Madeira
2 by-leaves

Preparation: The meat is pounded, skinned, some of the fat cut off, rubbed with salt and put in oven with 1 pt. boiling water, all spices and onion and roasted 2½ to 3 hours, basting it frequently.

For the gravy, skim off the fat, stir in the flour, stew a little while, then add some water, the wine or cream, and cook it well, strain and serve with the meat.

No. 3—BREADED LEG OF PORK.

Quantity for 10–15 Persons.

The meat is prepared the same way as described in No: 2, but ¾ hours before done, 8 cloves are stuck into it, ½ teaspoonful of sugar and 1 cup of rye bread crumbs roasted in butter are strewn over it. Cover it well with the bread crumbs by pressing it down with a knife, baste with drippings and roast ½ to ¾ hour longer.

For the gravy, stir in 1½ tablespoonfuls of flour, 1 glass red wine, 1½ cups of water; cook, strain and serve.

No. 4—BRAISED PORK ROAST.

Quantity for 6 Persons.

4 lbs. of pork
Salt, pepper
3 cloves
1 bay-leaf
1 small onion
2 tbsps. of flour
1½ pts. of water
2 tbsps. of white wine

Preparation: The meat is fried quickly to a light brown in 1 tablespoonful of lard and onion on the open fire, the flour is stirred in and browned a little. Now the water is poured on, salt and spices and wine added and then roasted in oven 2 to 2½ hours, turning and basting frequently.

For the gravy, skim off the fat, strain it and serve with the roast which must be a light brown.

No. 5—SOUR PORK ROAST.

Quantity for 6 Persons.

4 lbs. of pork shoulder
1 qt. vinegar
2 onions

6 pepper-corns
3 cloves
2 bay-leaves
1 handful of salt for pickling
1½ tbsps. of flour
2 cups of water
Salt
1 pinch of pepper
1 wineglass of red wine if you wish

Preparation: The meat is pounded and put into a jar or earthen dish with 1 qt. of vinegar, sliced onion, salt, cloves, peppers and bay-leaves and left in it for 2 days, turning it once or twice. When taken out to roast, put it into the oven with 1 cup of water, salt and pepper, also ½ of the onions that are in the vinegar, then roast 1¼ hours, basting frequently.

For the gravy, stir in the flour, stew a few minutes, add some water, the wine or ½ cup of cream, cook, pour over the roast. When this is done, strain the gravy and serve with the roast.

No. 6—PORK STEW.

Quantity for 6 Persons.

3 lbs. of pork
Salt
4 pepper-corns
2 cloves
1 bay-leaf
2½ qts. of water
½ onion

Preparation: The meat is washed and put on with 2½ qts. of cold water, onion, salt, spices and cooked slowly 2 to 2½ hours, covered. Skim the bouillon several times. Cut the meat in slices and arrange the vegetables around it. The bouillon may be used for boiling all kinds of vegetables, beans, peas and lentils.

No. 7—SALT PORK OR HIP-BONE FOR STEW.

Quantity for 6 Persons.

4 lbs. of salt pork or hip-bone
6 pepper-corns
2 cloves
1 bay-leaf
1 onion
3 qts. of water

Preparation: The salt pork or hip-bone is put on with 3 qts. of cold water, spices and onion, and cooked slowly for 3 hours. The pot must be well covered and ought to be an earthen dish. The broth will be jellied when cold and can be utilized for all kinds of headcheese.

No. 8—SMOKED HAM FOR COOKING.

Quantity for 15–20 Persons.

10 lbs. of ham
2 onions
6 cloves
2 bay-leaves
10 pepper-corns
Sufficient water

Preparation: The ham is soaked in water over night, then put it on the fire with cold water enough to cover it, onions and spices added. Cook it slowly in a large kettle for about 4 to 5 hours. Serve it warm with a Madeira gravy, or cold in slices.

No. 9—SMOKED HAM BOILED, BREADED WITH RYE BREAD CRUMBS.

Quantity for 15–20 Persons.

10 lbs. of ham
Sufficient water
Rye bread crumbs
1 tsp. of brown sugar
Cloves for larding

Preparation: The ham is soaked in water over night, then put on the fire with sufficient cold water to cover it, boil slowly for 4 hours. It will be quite done by this time. Put it on a platter, skin it and lard it where the skin has been removed with 30 to 40 cloves, sprinkle side with the sugar and thickly with the rye bread crumbs, then lay the ham into a pan and bake it in the oven for 1 hour. Serve with a Madeira gravy. This is a fine dish.

No. 10—HAM IN BURGUNDY WINE.

Quantity for 15–20 Persons.

10 lbs. of ham
2 bottles of Burgundy wine
2 small sliced onions
A leek
1 piece of thyme
1 piece of marjoram
¼ lb. of truffles
1 very large pig's bladder
2 tbsps. of butter
2½ tbsps. of flour
¼ pt. of Madeira
½ cup of bouillon
A cloth to tie up the ham
Water to boil in
¼ lb. of champignons

Preparation: The skin is cut off and the bones are taken out as well as possible. To the wine add the onion, the chopped leek, thyme and marjoram, then leave the ham in it for 24 hours, turning it over often. After that take it out, make a stuffing of truffles, champignons, 1 tablespoonful of butter, salt, pepper and ½ cup of bouillon mixed well and stuff the cavity left after removing the bone with it and sew it up. Clean the bladder well inside and outside, make a cut into it and put the stuffed ham inside, then pour in the wine with all its contents in which the ham has been lying for 24 hours, sew it up carefully. Then tie the whole into a white cloth and put it on the fire in cold water to boil for 4 to 5 hours slowly. After this, take the cloth off, open the suture, pour the fluid into a pot and put the ham into a pan.

Brown the butter and flour, add some of the ham fluid and Madeira, cook it well and add perhaps ½ teaspoonful of sugar, (better taste the gravy first). Fill some of this gravy over the ham and put it into the oven, roast for ¼ hour, then serve it with the gravy. Ham prepared in this way is very fine. If wine cannot be had, use Ginger Ale.

No. 11—FRIED HAM WITH EGGS.

Quantity for 6 Persons.

1 lb. raw ham sliced very thin
1½ pts. milk
12 eggs
1 pinch of salt and white pepper
⅛ lb. butter

Preparation: The ham is put in milk for 6 hours, then dry off the ham slices and fry them quickly in butter, put them on a platter and pour the butter over. In the meantime the eggs have been fried in butter with salt and pepper and now they are carefully placed on the ham.

Remarks: You need not put the ham into the milk and instead of ham you may take breakfast bacon. (Bacon and Eggs).

No. 12—BOILED HAM WITH NOODLES.

Quantity for 6 Persons.

1 lb. of boiled ham
Noodles made from 2 eggs
1 pt. milk
1 pinch of pepper
2–3 eggs
Some butter
Salt

Preparation: The ham is chopped fine. The noodles are cooked in salt water for ten minutes, then poured into a colander. Butter a casserole and put in a layer of noodles, then a layer of ham and repeat 2 or 3 times until all is in. The top layer must be noodles. The milk is well mixed with 2 or 3 eggs and very little salt and pepper and poured over the whole mass, a few pieces of butter on top and baked in oven slowly for 1 hour.

No. 13—BOILED HAM WITH MACARONI.

Quantity for 6 Persons.

1 lb. of boiled ham
½ lb. of macaroni
1 pt. of milk
Very little salt and pepper
Juice of 1 lemon
2 tbsps. of Parmesan cheese or Swiss cheese
2–3 eggs

Preparation: The ham is chopped fine and the macaroni broken in 2 inch pieces, boiled in salt water for ½ hour, then drain. Butter a casserole, put in a layer of macaroni and one of ham, repeat 2 or 3 times, with macaroni for the last layer. The milk is stirred well with eggs, salt, pepper, lemon juice and grated cheese and poured over the mass, then baked in the oven for one hour, after putting a few small pieces of butter on top. Serve in the casserole in which it was baked.

No. 14—BREADED HAM.

Quantity for 6 Persons.

1 lb. raw ham
⅛ lb. of butter or lard, good measure
2 cups of roll crumbs
1 pinch of salt
1½ pts. of milk
3 whites of eggs

Preparation: The ham is cut into ¼ inch thick slices and put into milk for 5 hours, then taken out, dried, salted, dipped into white of egg and then into roll crumbs mixed with the flour. Then it is fried in hot butter on both sides. These ham slices are nice to serve with vegetables.

No. 15—ROASTED PORK-FILLET.

Quantity for 6 Persons.

2–2½ lbs. of pork-fillet
⅛ lb. bacon for larding
Salt, pepper
1 tbsp. of flour
½ cup of sweet or sour cream
1 cup of water
2 tbsps. of butter or drippings

Preparation: The pork-fillets are pounded, the skin and most of the fat removed, then larded with bacon, salted and peppered. Put the fat which you cut off into a flat baking tin with some butter; into this heated lard and butter, put your fillets, baste often and let it roast in the oven 45 minutes to

1 hour. This depends on the size of the meat. 15 minutes before done, pour off some of the lard, stir in the flour to brown, then the water and gradually the cream, basting frequently. Strain the gravy and serve with the fillet.

No. 16—STUFFED PORK-FILLET CALLED MOCK DUCK.

Quantity for 6 Persons.

2 large fillets of 2½ lbs. or 4 small ones
⅛ lb. bacon for larding
Salt, pepper

For Stuffing.

½ lb. chopped pork
½ lb. chopped veal
2 eggs
2 tbsps. of butter for frying
½ tbsp. of butter
½ tbsp. of lemon juice
1 tbsp. of capers
Salt
1 pinch of pepper
½ tbsp. of flour
¼ cup of sweet or sour cream
1 cup of water

Preparation: The skin and fat are removed from the fillets and these pounded flat. Chopped pork and veal, eggs, ½ tablespoonful of butter, lemon juice, capers, salt and pepper are mixed well. This stuffing is placed between two fillets and these are then tied together with string or fastened together with toothpicks. If there are four fillets, put ½ of the stuffing on two and place the other two on top, then put bacon strips on top and fry them like No. 15, 1 to 1½ hours. Strain the gravy and serve with the fillets. This makes a very fine dish.

No. 17—ROASTED PORK CUTLETS.

Quantity for 6 Persons.

3 lbs. of pork cutlets
Salt, pepper
1 egg
1½ cups grated rolls
1 tbsp. of flour
1 clove
½ bay-leaf
¼ small onion
⅛ lb. of butter or lard
1 cup of water

Preparation: The pork cutlets are pounded, salted and peppered. The egg is beaten with a tablespoonful of milk and the cutlets dipped into this and then into the bread crumbs, then fried until light brown in hot butter or lard. This will require 15 minutes if they are ½ inch thick; if they are thicker, fry them for 20 minutes and place them on a hot platter.

If there is much fat in the pan, take some of it out and brown onion slices and flour in the remaining fat; add water, clove and bay-leaf, also salt and pepper, if necessary, and cook for 5 minutes. Strain the gravy and pour over cutlets or serve it separately.

No. 18—CHOPPED PORK CUTLETS.

Quantity for 6 Persons.

Preparation and ingredients are the same as in No. 17. The cutlets are chopped, carefully breaded and fried in butter about 8 to 10 minutes if the cutlets are ½ to ¾ inch thick.

No. 19—STEWED PORK CUTLETS.

Quantity for 6 Persons.

3 lbs. pork cutlets
Salt, pepper
½ cup of flour for dipping
1½ pts. of bouillon or water mixed with ½ tsp. of meat extract
2 cloves
1 bay-leaf
4 pepper-corns
½ sliced onion
1½–2 tbsps. of flour
1 wineglass Madeira or red wine
Juice of ¼ lemon
Butter

Preparation: The fat is cut off and the cutlets salted and peppered and dipped in flour, then fried quickly in hot butter on both sides. They are then taken out and put on a hot platter. The sliced onion and flour are browned in the drippings, bouillon, wine, spices, lemon juice, salt, 4 pepper-corns added, and cooked a while. The cutlets are then put into this gravy, covered and placed into the oven to stew one hour. When done, strain the gravy and serve with cutlets on the same platter.

No. 20—PORK KIDNEYS.

Quantity for 6 Persons.

1¾ lbs. pork kidneys
Salt, pepper
1½ tbsps. of flour
⅛ lb. of butter
1 pt. of bouillon
1½ tbsps. of vinegar

Preparation: The kidneys are cut crosswise into ¼ inch slices and fried in the hot butter 1 minute. Salt and pepper, stir in the flour, cook another minute and pour in bouillon and vinegar and cook 1 to 2 minutes more, stirring constantly. Have a good hot fire. The kidneys are tender when they do not look red any longer. If they cook too long, they get hard. Serve at once.

No. 21—PORK RAGOUT OR PORK PEPPER.

Quantity for 6 Persons.

2 lbs. of lean pork
1½ tbsps. of butter or lard
Salt, pepper
½ onion
2 cloves
1 bay-leaf
1½ tbsps. of vinegar or 1 wineglassful of red wine
3 tbsps. of flour
Some water or bouillon
½ cup of pig's blood if you can get it

Preparation: The meat is cut into 2½ inch squares. The butter and flour is browned, then bouillon or water, onion slices, spices and salt added and cooked a few minutes. Put in the meat and cook slowly ½ hour. Add the vinegar or red wine and continue to cook slowly until done, which will require ½ to 1 hour. Put the ragout in a warm dish and stir the blood into the gravy, strain and pour over the meat.

Remarks: You may omit the blood.

No. 22—MOCK RABBIT.

Quantity for 6 Persons.

1 lb. chopped pork
1 lb. chopped veal
1 lb. chopped beef

2 tbsps. of butter
3 eggs
2 soaked rolls
Juice of ½ lemon
1 tbsp. of capers
Salt
1 pinch of pepper
⅛ lb. of butter or lard for frying
½ tbsp. of flour
1 cup of water
1 cup of roll crumbs

Preparation: All the meat must be chopped very fine and mixed well with the roll from which the water has been well drained, eggs, 2 tablespoonfuls of butter, lemon juice, capers, salt, pepper, and 1 teaspoonful of grated onion. It is shaped into an oblong loaf and strewn with roll crumbs. The butter or lard is heated, the loaf of meat put in and baked in the oven one hour, basting frequently. Take out the mock rabbit carefully and put it on a platter. For the gravy, brown ½ tablespoonful of flour in the drippings, add the water, boil, and when done, strain and serve with the mock rabbit. You may also add ¼ cup of cream and some lemon juice to the gravy.

Remarks: You may also put 2 to 3 peeled, hard-boiled eggs into the loaf of meat, whole, before baking it. It is fine for slicing cold.

No. 23—STUFFED HOG'S HEAD.

Quantity for 10 Persons.

1 hog's head with ears
Salt
6 whole peppers
7 qts. of water for cooking
1 carrot
2 small onions
⅛ of a celery root

½ pt. of wine vinegar
4 cloves
2 bay-leaves

The Stuffing.

1 lb. chopped lean pork
1 lb. chopped lean veal
Salt, pepper
¼ lb. butter
3 eggs
Juice of ½ lemon
1 tsp. of grated onion
1 pinch of nutmeg.
2 soaked rolls

Extra.

1 lb. boiled beef tongue
½ lb. of boiled veal
½ lb. cooked pork
⅛ lb. truffles, cut in small pieces
½ lb. bacon
1 white cloth to tie up

Preparation: The head is cleaned well and split open lengthwise without cutting the skin. The bones are all taken out and the inside of the head is salted and peppered. The bones are split and put over the fire with the 7 qts. of water, the carrot, onion, celery, vinegar, cloves, and bay-leaf.

For the stuffing, mix well the chopped veal, salt, pepper, soaked rolls, ¼ lb. of butter, 3 eggs, grated onion, lemon juice, nutmeg and put the stuffing into the head, 1 inch thick, then make a layer of boiled tongue (½ inch slices), pork and veal. Then a thin layer of truffles. Repeat this, putting in stuffing, sliced meat and truffles alternately until both sides of the head are filled, sew it up, lay a piece of pork skin before the throat opening and sew it on. Tie up the whole head in the white cloth or sew it into the cloth and cook it 4 hours in the same water in which you have boiled the bones.

After it is done, leave it in the bouillon and cool it off; when it is nearly cold, place it on a board and weight it down. When it is cold, cut off the cloth and pick out all threads. Cut off a slice from the head so you can see the stuffing. Garnish by pinning a lemon slice into each eye with a toothpick, into the mouth place a bunch of parsley and around the head, green lettuce. This will make a fine cold supper or lunch. Serve a cold mustard gravy with it.

Remarks: The bouillon, after being boiled down considerably, may be used for aspic or head cheese.

No. 24—PORK RIBS AND SAUERKRAUT.

Quantity for 6 Persons.

3 lbs. salted pork ribs
1 lb. sauerkraut
¼ lb. butter
1 pinch of sugar
6 large, peeled and sliced apples
½ bottle of white wine

For Meat Dumplings.

¼ lb. chopped pork
¼ lb. chopped veal
1 egg
Salt, pepper
1 tbsp. of butter
¼ tbsp. of grated onion

Preparation: The pork ribs which have been salted for several days are cut into pieces, washed, dried and fried on both sides in hot butter, then put into a pot, the sauerkraut on top. (If the sauerkraut is too sour, soak it in water and drain). Add ¼ lb. of butter, apples, white wine and sugar, cover and cook slowly for 2 hours. When it gets too dry, pour in some water.

The Meat Dumplings: The chopped pork and veal, soaked roll, egg, 1 tablespoonful of butter and onion are mixed well. Shape into dumplings and fry well done in the butter in which you fried the ribs.

Arrange the sauerkraut in the middle of the platter, the ribs around it and the dumplings piled on top in a heap. Then serve. If you cannot get wine, omit it.

No. 25—SAUSAGE.

Quantity for 6 Persons.

2½ lbs. marbled pork
Salt
½ tsp. of cloves
½ tsp. of thyme
½ tsp. of white pepper

Preparation: The meat is ground three times or chopped very fine, then mixed well with the spices, filled into casings made from hog intestines and fried while fresh.

No. 26—FRIED SAUSAGE.

2½ lbs. of sausage
2 tbsps. of lard
1 small onion
Salt, pepper
1 cup of bouillon or water
½ tsp. of meat extract
1 tbsp. of flour

Preparation: The sausage is fried slowly in the hot lard until brown, then take it out and put the sliced onion into the same lard, add the flour, brown it, add water or bouillon, meat extract, if you have it, salt and pepper and cook. Pour this strained gravy over the sausage and serve.

No. 27—SAUSAGES.

Quantity for 6 Persons.

½ lb. lean pork
½ lb. fat pork from the loin
1 pinch of white pepper
2 casings of sheep intestines
Salt

Preparation: Meat and fat are chopped fine or ground 3 times, salted and peppered, filled into the casings and formed into lengths of sausages. You can improve the sausage by adding chopped truffles.

No. 28—FRIED SAUSAGES.

Quantity for 6 Persons.

1 lb. of sausages
2 whites of eggs
1 cup of grated rolls
Salt, drippings or butter
½ cup of flour

Preparation: The sausages are salted, dipped into white of egg, flour and bread crumbs and fried in hot drippings or butter to a nice brown color. They are nice with vegetables.

Remarks: You can prepare them like No. 26 and omit the bread crumbs.

No. 29—WHITE CABBAGE PIE WITH PORK.

Quantity for 6–8 Persons.

1 head of white cabbage
¾ lb. chopped pork
¾ lb. chopped beef
Salt
1 pinch of pepper
2 tbsps. of butter or drippings
2 eggs

Preparation: Remove the outer leaves and the core of the cabbage and boil until tender in salt water. Mix well the chopped pork and beef, butter, eggs, salt and pepper. Butter a pudding mold, drain the salt water from the cabbage and put in layers of cabbage and meat; repeat 3 times until all is in, the cabbage being on top, then close the mold, put it in a steamer over a kettle of boiling water and boil for 2 hours. Dump on a dish or platter after draining off the broth.

For the Gravy: Stir 5 rolled crackers with 1 tablespoonful of butter, salt, pepper, add the broth and boil. If it gets too thick, add some bouillon or water; stir in 2 yolks of eggs and serve with the pie.

Remarks: For the filling you may take pork only and for gravy thickening use flour instead of crackers.

No. 30—CABBAGE SAUSAGES.

Quantity for 6 Persons.

1 head of white cabbage
¾ lb. chopped pork
Salt, pepper
1 onion
Left over gravy or 1 pt. of false gravy
⅛ lb. of bacon

Preparation: The whole head of cabbage is boiled until half done in salt water. The outer leaves are then carefully taken off and some of the mixture of chopped pork, salt and pepper put on each leaf and the leaf is rolled or wrapped around it and tied with string. The bacon and onions are cut into small pieces and fried, then these little cabbage sausages are fried in it to a nice brown color. The gravy is poured over them, the pan is covered and the sausages stewed for 1½ to 2 hours, the string removed and served.

Remarks: If you have no gravy, make one by browning 1 tablespoonful of butter and 2 tablespoonfuls of flour and adding water or bouillon. Put in 3 tablespoonfuls of cream if you have it; salt, pepper and boil. If you have no bouillon, stir ½ teaspoonful of meat extract with water.

No. 31—SPANFERKEL OR ROAST LITTLE PIG.

Quantity for 8–10 Persons.

1 suckling pig
Salt
½ lb. of butter
¾ pt. of water
1 pinch of pepper

Preparation: The well washed and dressed pig is soaked in water for a few hours. The eyes are taken out and it is salted inside and outside. The fore and hind legs are bent under the pig and in this way it is placed into a pan with a tray on which it rests. Pour in some water and let it roast for 10 minutes. The butter is melted and the pig is brushed with it every 5 to 10 minutes. Gradually add water and cook it 1½ hours. Prick the skin several times so it will not blister; the butter will make the pig crisp. The drippings will be served as gravy or you can also serve a truffle, caper or tomato gravy with it.

No. 32—STUFFED SPANFERKEL OR ROAST LITTLE PIG.

Quantity for 8–10 Persons.

1 suckling pig
2 lbs. of sweet-sour apples
1 cup of dried currants
1 tbsp. of sugar
Salt
½ lb. of butter
½ cup seedless raisins

Preparation: The dressed and well washed pig is rubbed down with salt. The apples are peeled, cored and quartered, then mixed well with dried currants, raisins and sugar and stuffed into the pig which is then sewed up. Now bake just the same as No. 31.

Remarks: Sauerkraut and fried potatoes are good with it.

No. 33—SPANFERKEL A LA FRENCH STYLE.

Quantity for 8–10 Persons.

1 suckling pig
Liver, lungs and heart
½ lb. finely chopped pork
Salt, pepper
2 tbsps. of butter
1 egg

Preparation: The pig is washed well, dressed and rubbed with salt inside and outside. Liver, lungs and heart are chopped very fine and mixed well with butter, egg, salt, pepper and a few drops of lemon juice, then stuffed into the pig and this sewed up. The pig is brushed with fine salad oil and roasted slowly for 1½ to 2 hours. Water is added from time to time, garnish with lemon slices and serve with the gravy.

No. 34—MEAT SALTING AND PICKLING.

60 lbs. of meat
2 tbsps. of ground white pepper
2 lbs. of salt

The Brine.

4¼ lbs. of salt
⅛ lb. of saltpetre
Scant ½ lb. sugar
9 qts. of water

Preparation: Rub the meat with the 2 lbs. of salt until it all disappears and rub the joints and cuts with pepper. Then pack it into a barrel, the big pieces at the bottom, the small ones to fill in the cavities. After 2 days, make the brine by heating it, but not boiling, pour it on the meat and leave it on for 20 to 30 days according to the size of the pieces.

No. 35—PICKLED HAM.

1 raw ham, 10 to 12 lbs.
2¼ lbs. of salt
2 tbsps. of sugar
1/20 lb. of saltpetre

Preparation: Salt is heated in a pan and mixed well with saltpetre, then the ham is rubbed with it for 45 minutes. After this, put the ham into a barrel, well weighted. Pour the salt water, which it produces, over it often and turn the ham over several times. It may remain in the brine 5 to 6 weeks.

POULTRY AND GAME BIRDS.

POULTRY.

Cooked and Roasted Poultry.

Complete directions for utilizing Poultry Remnants.

THE CHICKEN.

The young chicken has a slender body and a delicate color. All young poultry has long legs, soft skin, feathers with oily quill that can be pulled out easily, small red comb, long claws and an elastic breast bone.

Old hens have a small, pale comb. If you wish to keep poultry, hang it up for a few days with the plumage, then pick it and dress it, stuff it with white paper, hang it up or wrap it in a clean cloth and put it on ice.

Poultry must not be cooked directly after slaughtering, because it will not get tender. According to the season it will keep 1–3 days.

A young chicken is roasted or fried. It is best when 8 to 16 weeks old. Old hens are good for cooking.

No. 1—ROAST SPRING CHICKEN.

Quantity for 6 Persons.

2–3 young spring chickens
Salt
¼ lb. of butter
1 tbsp. of flour
½ cup of sweet cream
½ pt. of water
3 thin slices of bacon

Preparation: The chicken is dressed, washed and dried well inside and outside and rubbed with salt.

Heart and liver may be put back into the chicken, gizzard and neck into the pan. The bacon slices are tied over the breast of the chicken, the pieces of butter put on top and then placed in the oven to roast one hour, basting it often until it is a golden yellow or light brown. Add water from time to time so that the butter will not get too brown. During the last 15 minutes put the cream, the flour and if necessary, water into the butter and let it simmer 15 minutes longer. Strain the gravy and serve with the chicken.

Remarks: You may leave off the bacon, but must baste the chicken every 5 minutes, because the breast gets dry very quickly.

No. 2—STUFFED ROAST CHICKENS.

Quantity for 6 Persons.

2 young chickens
2 slices of bacon to tie across the breast
¼ lb. butter for frying
Salt
½ tbsp. of flour
½ cup of cream
½ pt. of water

The Stuffing.

The heart, liver and gizzard
1 roll
1 tbsp. of butter
2 eggs
1 tsp. of finely chopped parsley
Salt
1 pinch of pepper
1 pinch of nutmeg
½ tbsp. of lemon juice

Preparation: The chickens are dressed, washed, dried and salted inside and outside. The stuffing made of finely chopped heart, liver, gizzard, from which the tough membrane has been removed, soaked roll, salt, pepper, parsley, nutmeg, butter, eggs and lemon juice, well mixed, is put into the chickens, the slices of bacon tied across the breast, the chickens sewed up and roasted exactly like No. 1.

Remarks: The stuffing may be made richer with ½ cup of chopped champignons and 3 truffles chopped fine.

No. 3—ANOTHER FORM OF STUFFED CHICKEN.

Quantity for 6 Persons.

2 young chickens
¼ lb. of butter
2 slices of bacon
½ cup of sweet cream
½ pt. of water
1 tbsp. of flour
Salt

The Stuffing.

2 tbsps. of butter
1 tbsp. of finely sliced onion
Heart, liver, gizzard chopped fine
2 eggs
Salt
1 pinch of pepper
1 pinch of nutmeg
1 tsp. of finely chopped parsley
1 roll soaked and the water pressed out

Preparation: The chickens are prepared as described in No. 1 and 2.

The stuffing is made by heating the butter and stewing the onion slices to a light yellow in it, then add the chopped heart, liver and gizzard and stew 5 minutes. Add the roll and all the other ingredients, stew another few minutes, stir in the eggs, stuff the chickens, sew them up, tie bacon across the breast and fry the same as in No. 1.

No. 4—STEWED CHICKEN WITH CHAMPIGNONS.

Quantity for 6 Persons.

2 young chickens
⅛ lb. of butter
2 tbsps. of flour
Bouillon or water
Salt
1 pinch of pepper
1½ wineglassful of red wine
½ pt. small champignons or 30 fresh, cleaned champignons
Juice of 1 lemon

Preparation: The chickens are dressed and washed and fried in ⅛ lb. of butter in the oven for 15 minutes, basting them several times. After this time, stir into the butter the 2 tablespoonfuls of flour, add bouillon or water, salt, pepper, wine and champignons, cover the pot or pan, stew the chickens for 1 hour. Lastly put in the lemon juice and serve the chickens and gravy on one platter.

No. 5—OLD OR YOUNG CHICKEN WITH RICE.

Quantity for 6 Persons.

1 old chicken or 2 young ones
3 qts. of water
Salt
¾ cup of rice

Water and chicken bouillon
½ tbsp. of fresh butter
2 slices of onion

For the Gravy.

1 tbsp. of butter
2 tbsps. of flour
½ wineglassful of white wine
2 yolks of eggs
Chicken bouillon

Preparation: The chickens are dressed, washed and boiled until tender in 3 qts. of water, the salt and onion slices. Boil a young chicken 45 minutes, old chicken 2–3 hours, according to its age. In the meantime, cook the rice in a double boiler with a few cups of bouillon and a little salt. When the rice is done, stir in a piece of fresh butter. Do not cook it too mushy.

The Gravy: Stir 1 tablespoonful of butter and 2 of flour, add some of the chicken broth, cook a few minutes till it thickens, add the white wine and stir in the 2 yolks of eggs.

The chickens are carved in nice pieces and placed in a heap in the middle of the platter, the rice around it and the gravy poured over the meat; or leave the chicken whole, place the rice around and serve the gravy separately.

Remarks: The gravy may be prepared without wine.

No. 6—CHICKEN PIE.

Quantity for 6 Persons.

2 young chickens or 1 old one
3 qts. of water
Salt
1 tbsp. of butter
1½ tbsps. of flour

The Paste.

½ lb. of butter and lard, more butter than lard or butter only
½ lb. of flour, good measure
1½ tumblerfuls of water

Preparation: The chickens are dressed, washed and put to boil in the water and salt. Young chicken will be tender in 45 minutes, old chicken in 2 to 3 hours.

The Paste: Butter and lard must be very cold. Cut it into the flour and add the very cold water, mix lightly and roll one-half of it out in ¼ inch thick layer. The paste must be dry; the butter must be visible after rolling. Put this layer into a baking dish, cut up the chickens, put the pieces into the dish, pour in the bouillon so that meat and broth are even. Roll the other half of the paste, make a few cuts into it and cover the pie, trimming off the edge neatly. Bake in the oven 1 hour to a golden yellow color. Leave only enough broth for the gravy. Stir into the broth 1 tablespoonful of butter, 1½ of flour, cook, strain and serve with the pie.

Cabbage salad and fresh boiled potatoes go nicely with it.

No. 7—PUFF PASTE PATTIES, FILLED WITH CHICKEN RAGOUT.

Quantity for 6 Persons.

1 small young chicken
Salt
1½ qts. of water

For the Gravy.

2 tbsps. of butter
2 tbsps. of flour
Chicken broth
½ wineglassful of white wine

½ cup sweet cream
Juice of ½ lemon
Salt
1 pinch of white pepper
½ pt. can champignons

The Paste.

½ lb. very cold fresh butter
½ lb. flour
1 tbsp. of strong brandy
½ of an egg
¼ pt. very cold water

Preparation: The chicken is prepared well and cooked until tender in 1½ qts. of salt water, then cut up into very small pieces.

The Gravy: Melt the butter, stir in the flour, fill up with chicken broth, add cream and wine, cook till it thickens, put in the chopped champignons and the meat, season with salt and pepper, fill hot into the ready baked patties. Then bake in moderately hot oven for about 10 minutes and serve immediately.

Bake the patties according to No. 39, Chapter 3, Veal Sweetbread Patties.

No. 8—CHICKEN RAGOUT IN SHELLS OR OTHER SMALL MOLDS.

Quantity for 6 Persons.

1¼ lbs. of cooked chicken
2 tbsps. of butter
2 tbsps. of flour
Some bouillon
½ wineglassful of white wine
Juice of ½ lemon

Salt
1 pinch of pepper
½ cup. of sweet cream

Preparation: The chicken meat is cut up into small pieces. Butter is melted and flour stirred in, broth, cream and white wine added, seasoned with salt, pepper and lemon juice, cooked and filled into the shells or other small molds. Sprinkle with bread crumbs, place pieces of butter on top and bake in oven to a nice brown color.

Remarks: This ragout may be improved with ½ pt. of finely chopped champignons and 4 truffles also chopped fine. This chicken ragout in shells makes an excellent side dish.

No. 9—CHICKEN CROQUETTES.

The preparation and ingredients are the same as in No. 31, Veal Croquettes, or No. 30, Veal Sweetbread Croquettes. See Chapter 3.

No. 10—FINE CHICKEN FRICASSEE.

Quantity for 6–8 Persons.

2 young chickens
Salt
¼ lb. of butter

For the Gravy.

2½—3 tbsps. of flour
½ pt. sweet or sour cream
Bouillon or water
½ pt. champignons
6 sliced truffles
½ cup champignon juice
1 wineglassful of Madeira or white wine

Salt
1 pinch of white pepper
Some lemon juice

Preparation: The chickens are dressed and washed, fried light brown in ¼ lb. of butter, and, when well done, carved.

For the gravy, stir into the drippings the flour, water or bouillon, cream, wine, champignons, juice and cook well. The gravy ought to be quite thick and light yellow, strain and season it with lemon juice, salt, if necessary, some pepper, and put in the whole champignons and the sliced truffles.

The chicken should be so carved that the meat will not fall from the bones and should be kept very hot. Put the meat on a platter and pour the gravy over it. Garnish the rim with puff paste scallops and small meat dumplings.

The dumplings are made by chopping the chicken liver, heart and gizzard, mixing it well with ½ soaked roll, salt, pepper, 1 egg, ½ teaspoonful of lemon juice. Fry the mixture in 1 tablespoonful of butter; when cool, form small dumplings and fry them a light brown in very little butter. This is a very fine dish.

No. 11—VIENNA BAKED CHICKEN.

Quantity for 6 Persons.

3 young, fresh chickens
Salt
⅛ lb. of flour
2½ cups of bread crumbs
3 lbs. of lard for frying
1 lemon for garnishing
1–2 eggs

Preparation: The chickens are killed, dressed, washed, dried and prepared at once. Cut the chickens in half, salt them, dip them first into flour, then in beaten egg and then in bread crumbs. The lard is heated in an iron pot or kettle and the pieces of chicken placed into it carefully, one at a time, so as not to cool the fat too much and that the crumbs may not fall off. Bake them to a nice brown color. After the crust is hard, let them cook more slowly until well done. Then put on paper to drain, strew fine salt over the pieces and put on a platter after which they may be garnished with lemon slices.

No. 12—CHICKEN OR PIGEON CUTLET.

Quantity for 6 Persons.

3 young chickens or 6 young pigeons
Salt
1 pinch of pepper
2 eggs
Some flour
1½ cups of roll crumbs
Lemon
¼ lb. of butter

Preparation: The birds are dressed, washed and skinned. Each breast is quartered and pounded a little, on each piece fasten a scraped wingbone and season with salt and pepper.

Beat the egg well with 1½ tablespoonfuls of drawn butter, dip in the cutlets and then into roll crumbs, mixed with 2 tablespoonfuls of flour, then fry in butter 8 to 10 minutes, turning them often. With asparagus these poultry cutlets are very fine.

Remarks: The scraps of poultry may be utilized for soup, croquettes or fricassee.

No. 13—CHICKEN PIE, ENGLISH STYLE.

Quantity for 6–8 Persons.

2 young chickens
¾ lb. of veal steak
½ lb. of boiled ham
2 tbsps. of chopped parsley
3 hard-boiled eggs
2 tbsps. of flour
1 pt. of water or bouillon
Salt
1 pinch of pepper
1 tbsp. of butter

Preparation: The paste is made the same as the chicken pie in No. 6.

The chickens are prepared as in No. 6, the meat removed from the bones and cut into ¼ inch slices, the ham and veal too. The baking dish is lined with the paste and filled with alternate layers of meat, salted and peppered, chopped parsley and champignons and the yolks of eggs put in whole.

The tablespoonful of butter and 2 of flour are browned a little, broth or water added, stewed, and this poured over the meat. Cover with the paste as described in No. 6, then bake in the oven slowly for 1¾ hours. The pie may be eaten cold. Use no flour for the gravy, but clear broth.

No. 14—PIGEON PIE, ENGLISH STYLE.

Quantity for 6 Persons.

4 pigeons
¾ lb. of beefsteak
6 hard-boiled eggs, the yolks only
¼ pt. finely chopped champignons
¼ lb. of butter
1½ tbsps. of flour
¾ pt. of bouillon
Salt
1 pinch of pepper

2 tbsps. of finely chopped parsley
¼ onion

Prepare the pie crust as described in No. 6. See Chicken Pie.

Preparation: The pigeons are dressed, washed and fried in the butter for ½ hour, then cut in halves. Fry the steak, which has been cut into small pieces and the fat taken off, in the same butter for 10 minutes. Prepare a baking dish with the crust as described in No. 6, put in the meat, salted and peppered, parsley and champignons and place the yolks of eggs here and there between the meat. Slice the ¼ onion and brown together with the flour in the drippings, add the bouillon, stew, strain and pour over the meat, then cover with crust according to No. 6 and bake in the oven 1¼ hours.

Remarks: For the crust, use butter only.

No. 15—FRIED PIGEON.

Quantity for 6 Persons.

6 young pigeons
¼ lb. of butter
1 cup of cream
½ cup of water
1 tbsp. of flour

Preparation: The pigeons are dressed, washed, salted inside and outside. Heat the butter and fry the pigeons light brown on every side, basting with spoonfuls of water and cream. During the last ten minutes stir in the flour and add some more water if necessary, strain the gravy. On the stove it requires 1½ hours to fry the pigeons, to roast in the oven only one hour.

No. 16—STUFFED FRIED PIGEONS.

Quantity for 6 Persons.

6 young pigeons
¼ lb. of butter
½ cup of cream
1 cup of water
1 tbsp. of flour.

For the Stuffing.

2 soaked rolls
Chopped heart, liver, gizzard
1 tbsp. of butter
2 eggs
¼ pt. finely chopped champignons
4 truffles, chopped
Salt, pepper
1 tsp. of chopped parsley.

Preparation: The pigeons are dressed, washed and salted inside and outside.

The stuffing is made by mixing well the chopped liver, heart and gizzard from which the inner membrane has been removed with all the other ingredients. Stuff the pigeons with it, sew them, up and fry them as stated in [No. 15](); prepare the gravy likewise.

Remarks: You may make the stuffing more simply by omitting the champignons and truffles.

No. 17—FRIED PIGEONS WITH SWEET STUFFING.

4 pigeons
3 soaked rolls
½ cup of ground almonds
½ cup of dried currants
2 eggs
3 tbsps. of sugar
1 pinch of salt

⅛ lb. of butter

Preparation: The butter is melted, and the soaked rolls stirred in and sautéed or dry fried. The almonds are scalded, skinned and ground and added with the rest of the ingredients. The pigeons are stuffed and prepared same as in No. 15.

No. 18—ROAST TURKEY.

Quantity for 10–15 Persons.

1 turkey weighing 8 to 10 pounds
½ lb. of butter
Salt
1 cup of cream
2 cups of water
2 tbsps. of flour
1 pinch of white pepper

Preparation: The turkey is dressed and soaked in cold water 30 minutes, then dried and seasoned with pepper and salt inside and outside. The butter is placed in bits on the turkey and if it is a young turkey, roast it in the oven 2 hours, basting frequently with cream and water.

For the gravy, brown the flour in the drippings, add water, cook, strain and serve with the turkey.

If the turkey is older it will require 3 hours to cook it well, and it is best to cover it so it will not get too brown. To prevent the butter from getting too dark, add water from time to time.

Remarks: The leavings may be utilized in many ways. Turkey ragout in shells, see No. 8 for Chicken ragout in shells; Turkey croquettes, see No. 31. or No. 30, Chapter 3, Veal and veal sweetbread croquettes; Turkey pie, see No. 6, Chicken pie. The bones make a good soup.

No. 19—ROASTED AND STUFFED TURKEY.

Quantity for 10–15 Persons.

The Stuffing.

3 soaked rolls
Chopped liver, heart and gizzard
Salt, pepper
2 tbsps. of butter
1 tbsp. of chopped parsley
1 tsp. of lemon juice

Preparation: Mix these ingredients well, stuff the turkey with the mixture and roast as directed in No. 18. Prepare the gravy the same as in No. 18.

The Goose.

The young goose or gosling has a soft gullet, a pale yellow bill and feet with pointed claws. The bill and feet of old geese are reddish yellow. The color of the skin must be white, not purple or blue.

The time for fat geese is from October to January.

No. 20—ROASTED YOUNG GOOSE.

Quantity for 6 Persons.

1 young goose
Salt
6 pepper-corns
⅛ lb. of butter
½ onion, sliced
2 tbsps. of flour
1 pt. cold water

Preparation: The goose is cleaned and dressed. The wings, neck, head and feet chopped off. The fat is trimmed off, even from the bowels, and is soaked in water separately from the meat. The goose is washed and left to soak in cold water for 15 minutes, then dried and rubbed with salt inside and outside. Put it into the oven with 1 pt. of water, sliced onion and pepper-corns. When the water is boiled down pretty much, baste the goose frequently with browned butter. A young goose will be done in 1½ hours. It should be of a light brown color and very crisp. Sprinkle a tablespoonful of cold water over it to make it crisp.

Now prepare the gravy by stirring the flour into the drippings, cook it a few minutes and add water. Cook well, strain and serve with the goose.

No. 21—FAT GOOSE STUFFED WITH APPLES.

Quantity for 7–9 Persons.

1 goose, 7 to 8 lbs.
Salt
½ sliced onion
1½ pts. of water
6 pepper-corns

The Gravy.

2 tbsps. of flour
Some water

The Stuffing.

1½ lbs. peeled, quartered apples
½ cup currants

Preparation; The goose is prepared as described in the previous number, washed and salted inside and outside.

The prepared apples are mixed well with the currants and stuffed into the goose, which is then sewed up. The goose is put into the oven in a covered roasting pan with the water, sliced onion and pepper-corns, and roasted for 1 hour. After that time, remove the cover, baste with the drippings every 10 to 15 minutes, and if the water boils down, add spoonfuls of it so the fat will not get too brown. It may require from 2 to 3 hours roasting before the goose is well done and crisp. Sprinkle a tablespoonful of cold water over the skin to make it more crisp. Then serve.

For the gravy, pour off nearly all of the grease and prepare as described in No. 20. If there is very much grease from the goose, skim some of it off while roasting.

No. 22—FAT GOOSE STUFFED WITH CHESTNUTS.

Quantity for 7–9 Persons.

The Stuffing.

2 lbs. of chestnuts, the liver
1 pinch of salt
1 pinch of pepper
3 tbsps. of butter
1 tsp. of sugar
Some water

Preparation: The preparation and ingredients for goose and gravy are the same as in No. 21. The chestnuts are put into the oven; when the shells burst take them out, peel them at once and chop them fine. Put them into a kettle over the fire with water, butter, 1 pinch of salt and 1 of pepper and sugar and cook until well done, then put in the chopped goose liver, stuff the goose with this mixture and sew it up. Prepare the roast and gravy as directed in No. 21.

No. 23—FRIED GOOSE LIVER.

Quantity for 7–9 Persons.

1 goose liver
½ pt. milk and water
1 egg
Some flour
Salt
1 pinch of pepper
1 piece of butter for frying
¼ cup of goose gravy or ¼ tablespoonful of flour mixed with broth

Preparation: Carefully remove the gall from the liver and put the liver into milk diluted with water for 2 hours, dry it well, salt and pepper, dip into beaten egg, then into flour. Heat the butter and fry the liver 5 minutes to a light brown, turning it several times. Serve on a hot platter. For the gravy, brown ¼ tablespoonful of flour in the butter, add broth or water, cook well and serve with the liver.

No. 24—GOOSE GIBLETS.

Quantity for 2–3 Persons.

From one goose the heart, gizzard, head, wings, feet and neck
1 qt. of water
Salt
4 pepper-corns
2 cloves
1 bay-leaf
½ onion, sliced

For the Gravy.

2 tbsps. of butter
3 tbsps. of flour
Bouillon
1 yolk of egg

Preparation: The feet are scalded and skinned, the gizzard emptied and also scalded and skinned, the gullet cut from the neck, the eyes taken out, wings, neck and head well cleaned and singed. Now put all this in a kettle over the fire with the water, onion, salt, peppers, cloves, bay-leaf and cook until tender.

For the gravy, melt the butter, stir in the flour, cook and add the goose broth. The gravy must be smooth; stir into it one yolk of egg and pour it on the giblets. Serve in a deep dish.

Fresh, peeled potatoes are good with it.

Remarks: You may also utilize these goose giblets for soup and put in small potatoes.

No. 25—GOOSE LIVER PIE.

Quantity for 6 Persons.

3 large goose livers
¾ lb. veal
¾ lb. fat pork
6 truffles
1½ lemon
⅛ lb. of butter
⅔ pt. of bouillon
2 tbsps. of Madeira or red wine
Salt, pepper
3 yolks of eggs
1 tsp. of grated onion
Bacon slices to line the pan
4 tbsps. of flour

Preparation: Two of the goose livers are larded with oblong slices of peeled truffles. Drip the juice from 1½ lemons on the livers and let stand for several hours.

The ⅛ lb. of butter is heated, mixed with the flour, salt and pepper and ¾ pt. of broth and Madeira added. The finely chopped or ground veal and pork are stirred into the thick gravy. The one goose liver is chopped, fried 2 minutes in 2 tablespoonfuls of butter and the onion, salted and peppered and mixed into the filling. Fill all this into a deep baking pan or mold lined with bacon slices so that it makes 2 to 3 layers of stuffing, alternating with slices of goose liver. Cover with slices of bacon, set in steamer over a kettle of boiling water and boil for 1½ hours or bake in oven for 1 hour.

A truffle or Madeira gravy may be served with it.

No. 26—GOOSE LIVER PUDDING.

Quantity for 6 Persons.

3 large goose livers
¼ lb. of bacon
3 tbsps. of butter
3 rolls soaked in milk
¼ onion
3 eggs
3 tbsps. grated Parmesan cheese
3 tbsps. of cream
Salt, pepper
Butter for the mold

Preparation: Liver and bacon are chopped fine. Fry the butter, grated onion, and the roll a few minutes, then put in the chopped liver and bacon, salt, pepper, cheese, cream, 3 yolks of eggs, the beaten whites and mix well. Put into a buttered mold, set in a steamer over a kettle of boiling water and boil for one hour, dump it on a plate and serve with a hot, brown gravy. This pudding may be made of duck liver as well; truffles may be added to make it richer. It makes a fine dish garnished with roasted blackbirds.

No. 27—ROASTED WILD GOOSE.

Quantity for 6 Persons.

1 wild, young goose
8 large, sour apples
2 tbsps. of butter
1 pinch of salt and pepper
3 large onions

For Roasting.

⅛ lb. of butter
Some water
Some slices of bacon

The Gravy.

1½ tbsps. of flour
1 cup of broth

Preparation: Wild geese are usually very tough, therefore take a young goose only. Clean and dress it well, let it soak in water for ½ hour, dry it and salt it inside and outside.

The filling or stuffing is made by heating the butter, chopping the scalded onion and put into the butter together with the peeled and sliced apples, cut into ⅛ths. Let these cook half done, then add 1 pinch of white pepper, salt and 2 pulverized cloves, fill the goose with this and sew it up.

Tie the slices of bacon across the breast of the goose and put into the oven with the water and ⅛ lb. of butter, basting it frequently. When the gravy gets too brown add more water. After it is well cooked, take off the string and bacon and serve it.

The Gravy: Stir some flour into the broth, add water or more broth, cook a few minutes, strain and serve.

No. 28—SMOKED GOOSE BREAST.

The breast of one goose
⅜ lb. of salt
1 tsp. of saltpetre
1 tbsp. of sugar

Preparation: The breast is cut from an undressed goose. Cut off the legs and the meat off the breast down to the bone. Be careful not to injure the outer skin. The small fillets are separated from the breast and it is rubbed well with ½ the quantity of salt, which has been mixed with the saltpetre and sugar until it dissolves. Replace the small fillets after salting them also, fold, and sew up the breast. Salt it well on the outside and place into a crock for 7 days, turning it twice a day and basting it well with the brine that collects. On the eighth day wrap in paper, place it between two boards, well weighted, and draw a string through the top end of fat and skin by which to hang it up. Hang it into a smoke house in medium smoke for 8 to 10 days. Then place again between two boards weighted down for a few days. By this process the fat becomes white and hard and the meat keeps better.

The Duck.

When the duck is 6 months old it makes the finest roast, but you may roast it up to a year old. The best time for duck is from August to the beginning of December.

No. 29—ROAST DUCK.

Quantity for 6–8 Persons.

2 ducks
Salt
1 pinch of pepper
Some butter for roasting
10–12 sweet-sour apples
1 cup currants

2 tbsps. of flour
1½ cups of water

Preparation: The duck is dressed, neck, wings and feet cut off and it is washed, dried and salted inside and outside. The apples are peeled, quartered, mixed well with the currants, filled into the duck and this sewed up. Put it into a pan with the water, 2 tbsps. butter, and roast for 1½ hours, basting frequently.

For the Gravy: If there is too much grease, pour some of it off, stir in the flour, brown it a little, add water, cook well, strain and serve with the duck.

No. 30—ANOTHER FORM OF STUFFED DUCK.

Quantity for 6–8 Persons.

2 ducks
Salt
1 pinch of pepper
2 tbsps. of butter for roast

The Stuffing.

Chopped heart, liver and gizzard
3 rolls, soaked
3 eggs
1 tbsp. of finely chopped parsley
1 tbsp. of lemon juice
Salt, pepper
⅛ onion chopped finely
1 tbsp. of butter

For the Gravy.

2 tbsps. of flour
1½ cups of water

Preparation: The ducks are dressed after cutting off neck, wings and feet, then washed and salted and strewn with 1 pinch of pepper inside and outside.

The stuffing is made of chopped liver, heart, gizzard, mixed with all the other ingredients and put into the ducks, which are then sewed up and treated just the same as described in No. 29.

Prepare the gravy as given in No. 29.

No. 31—FRIED DUCK LIVER.

This is prepared the same as described in No. 23.

No. 32—GOOSE AND DUCK SCHWARZ-SAUER.

Black Soup.

Quantity for 4 Persons.

Giblets of 1 goose or duck
Salt
¼ lb. prunes
¼ cup of sugar
1 small stick of cinnamon
½ lb. of peeled apples or pears
2 cloves
4 pepper-corns
Scant 1 pt. of goose or duck blood
1½ tbsps. of vinegar
1½ qts. of water
2 tbsps. of flour

Preparation: Neck, head, feet, wings, heart and gizzard are cleaned well and cooked until tender in 1 qt. of water with salt, pepper and 2 cloves. The prunes and quartered apples or pears are cooked until done in ½ qt. of water. The blood is stirred with the flour into ½ of the broth from the giblets and poured back on again. The chopped fruit added, then seasoned with vinegar and sugar and brought to boil, stirring constantly. It must not coagulate.

THE GAME BIRDS.
THE PHEASANT.

One can recognize the young bird by its less developed spurs and flexible bones. The pheasant may become 5 to 10 years old. Freshly shot pheasants are not good to eat because the meat is dry and hard. In winter the bird may be left hanging with its feathers for 2 to 3 weeks.

No. 33—FRIED PHEASANT.

Quantity for 6 Persons.

1 pheasant
Salt
⅛ lb. of butter
2 thin slices of bacon to tie across the breast
1½ tbsps. of flour
1 cup of water
½ pt. sweet or sour cream

Preparation: The young pheasant is dressed, carefully washed and dried, then salted inside and outside and the liver put back into the bird with a piece of butter. The slices of bacon are tied across the breast.

Put the pheasant into the oven with ⅛ lb. of butter, baste it frequently and roast to a golden yellow. After 30 minutes, baste frequently with the cream and water by spoonfuls. It will require 1 to 1½ hours to cook it well done. Before serving, remove the bacon slices.

Into the drippings stir the flour, brown it, if necessary add more water, cook and strain and serve the gravy with the bird.

No. 34—FRIED OLD PHEASANT.

The preparation is just the same as the one under No. 33, with the exception that it requires from 2½ to 3 hours to cook the bird well done, therefore take a little more cream and water for basting and cover the roasting pan during part of the time to keep the bird from getting too dark.

No. 35—PHEASANT PATTIES.

In Shells or Other Small Molds.

Quantity for 6–8 Persons.

½ lb. roasted pheasant meat
3 tbsps. of butter
3 tbsps. of flour
Pheasant broth from bones
½ wineglassful of white wine
3 chopped truffles
½ cup of chopped champignons
Salt
1 pinch of pepper
Some butter for the molds
2 eggs

Preparation: The skin is removed from the meat. The meat, truffles and champignons are chopped fine. The bones are put on the fire with 2 qts of water, salt, a small piece of onion and boiled down to ½ qt. of bouillon. Then the gravy is made by heating the 3 tablespoonfuls of butter and the same quantity of flour stirred in to brown, ½ qt. of bouillon added and cooked. Season with salt and pepper, add white wine, meat, truffles and champignons and stir in the 2 yolks of eggs. Beat the whites of eggs and stir lightly into the mixture. When this is done, fill the shells or buttered molds with the filling and bake in the oven to a nice brown color.

Remarks: Truffles and champignons may be omitted.

No. 36—STEWED PHEASANT.

Quantity for 6 Persons.

1 pheasant
Salt
Broth cooked from neck, wings, gizzard, liver, heart
1 large onion, sliced
6 pepper-corns
1 small carrot, sliced
2–3 wineglassfuls of white wine or sherry
3 tbsps. of butter
3 tbsps. of flour
3 tomatoes, sliced
2 bay-leaves

Preparation: The pheasant is cleaned, dressed, put into a stewpot with 3 tablespoonfuls of butter, fried a little on all sides, the flour stirred in and then enough broth added to cover the bird. Put in the rest of the ingredients named above and roast slowly in the oven for 2 to 2½ hours.

Strain the gravy through a fine sieve and serve with the pheasant.

No. 37—PHEASANT PIE.

Quantity for 8–10 Persons.

2 young pheasants
⅛ lb. of butter
Salt
1½ qts. broth from bones
½ wineglassful of Madeira
Juice of ½ lemon
½ pt. of champignons
1 small can of truffles

Pie Contents.

Liver, heart, gizzard, chopped fine
2½ soaked rolls
3 eggs
Salt
1 pinch of pepper
1 tbsp. of butter
1 tsp. of chopped onion

Preparation: The pheasants are cleaned, dressed and fried in oven for 20 minutes with ⅛ lb. of butter. The meat is then removed from the bones and a good qt. of broth is made from the latter, seasoned with Madeira, salt, lemon juice. The champignons are quartered and the truffles sliced; liver, heart, gizzard chopped fine, the rolls, salt, pepper, and yolk of egg stirred in. The onions are cooked a little in the drippings and the whole mixture added and stewed a little while. The whites of eggs are beaten and stirred into the mixture after it has cooled. Now butter your dish and put in one-half of the giblet filling as the bottom layer, then one layer of meat, then champignons and truffles, and so on until all the meat, champignons and truffles have been used. The broth is poured over the whole, the other half of the giblet filling put on the top and it is now baked in the oven for 1¼ hours. Serve it in the dish or casserole.

No. 38—RED GROUSE AND GUINEA HEN.

Quantity for 6 Persons.

3 red grouse or 3 guinea hens
⅛ lb. of butter
Salt
½ pt. of cream
1½ tbsps. of flour
1 cupful of water
Bacon slices to tie across the breast

Preparation: The preparation is the same as No. 33, Pheasant. It also requires 1 to 1½ hours for cooking.

Remarks: Grouse gets very tender when kept in buttermilk over night.

No. 39—GROUSE PIE.

Quantity for 14 Persons.

3 red grouse
Buttermilk
⅛ lb. of butter
Salt

Pie Filling.

¾ lb. beef with bones
¾ lb. lean pork
1 small can of truffles
1 pt. can champignons
5 soaked rolls

4 eggs
3 tbsps. of butter
Juice of ½ lemon
1 tsp. of grated onions
1 glass Madeira
Salt
1 pinch of pepper

Preparation: The grouse must be well hung; dress, salt and bake in hot oven with ⅛ lb. of butter for one hour, basting frequently. If buttermilk is to be obtained, put the grouse in buttermilk for 24 hours before baking. After frying, cut off the breasts and divide them into ⅛ths. The other meat is cut from the bones and chopped fine, also the beef and pork. The soaked rolls are sautéed or dry fried in 3 tablespoonfuls of butter and 4 eggs stirred into them. Now add grouse meat, beef, pork, salt, pepper, juice of ½ lemon, 1 wineglassful of Madeira, 1 teaspoonful of grated onion and mix well. The bones of the birds and beef are put on the fire with the champignon and truffle juice and boiled down to ½ qt. of broth, half of which is stirred into the filling.

Butter your dish or casserole and after lining it with paste, put in a layer of filling, then one of meat, strewing on some chopped champignons and truffles. Pour in the other ½ of the broth, cover with paste and bake in oven 1¼ hours to a nice brown color. Serve with a Madeira gravy.

The paste is made by mixing lightly ¼ lb. of flour with ¼ lb. of cold butter, ½ glassful of cold water and 1 teaspoonful of brandy, then rolled out.

Remarks: These pies may be made of pheasants, heath cocks or hazel hens, snow hens, snipes, quails and partridges.

No. 40—FRIED PARTRIDGES.

Quantity for 6 Persons.

6 young partridges
Salt
Bacon slices

¼ lb. of butter
½ pt. sour cream
1 tbsp. flour
Some water

Preparation: After the birds have been cleaned, singed, dressed, wiped out and salted, tie the bacon slices around them, put them into a pan, pour on the hot butter and fry them for ½ hour, basting frequently and adding the cream by spoonfuls. When well done, take off the bacon and serve with the following gravy. In the drippings, brown 1 tablespoonful of flour, add a little water if necessary, cook, strain and serve. A little white wine may be added to the gravy.

No. 41—PARTRIDGE WITH SAUERKRAUT.

Quantity for 6 Persons.

2 young partridges
1½ lbs. of sauerkraut
2 tbsps. of butter
2 thin slices of bacon
1 wineglassful of white wine
Water for the sauerkraut
1 tbsp. of flour
1 apple

Preparation: The partridges are cleaned, singed, dressed and wiped out, bacon slices tied on and fried in 2 tablespoonfuls of butter for 15 minutes. If the sauerkraut is too sour, soak it in water a while, drain, then put it on the stove with the partridges and a little water, white wine, sliced apple, cover and stew slowly for 2 hours. When the birds are tender, take off the bacon, stir a little flour into the sauerkraut; cook for a few minutes and serve with the birds.

No. 42—FINE RAGOUT OF PARTRIDGE.

Quantity for 6 Persons.

3 young partridges
1 pint champignons
1 piece of bacon for larding
½ lb. goose liver or calf sweetbreads
Salt

For the Gravy.

3 tbsps. of butter
3 tbsps. of flour
Broth from the bones
3 tbsps. of red wine
3 tbsps. of Madeira
1 tsp. of meat extract
The champignon juice
3 pepper-corns
Salt
1 pinch of sugar

For the Dumplings.

Heart, liver, gizzard, some meat from the bones
1 soaked roll
2 eggs
Salt, pepper
Some butter to fry the dumplings
A few slices of toasted wheat bread
1 tbsp. of butter

Preparation: The partridges are well prepared. Cut off the breast and drum sticks and all other meat from the bones. The latter are cracked, put on the fire with 3 tablespoonfuls of butter and flour, fried quickly, then 1½ qts. of water, the champignon juice, some salt, 3 pepper-corns added and boiled slowly for 2 hours to make ½ to ¾ qt. of broth. Season this broth with red wine, Madeira, meat extract, sugar and strain it. Lard the breasts and fry them and the drum sticks or legs in butter. Cover and stew slowly for ½ hour until done. Drip the lemon juice on the goose liver, salt it and fry it in butter. If you have sweetbreads instead of goose liver, parboil in salt water for 10 minutes, remove the skin, drip on lemon juice and fry in butter.

To make the dumplings, chop the liver, heart, gizzard and meat from the bones very fine and mix well with the soaked roll, one egg, butter, salt, pepper, some chopped champignons and shape into dumplings. Fry these light brown in butter or cook 10 minutes in broth.

Toast the wheat bread slices, cut each partridge breast into 4 pieces, also the goose liver or sweetbreads. Place the toast on a hot platter, then on this the meat, breast, legs and the goose liver or sweetbreads. Put the champignons into the gravy and pour hot over the meat. Garnish the dish with the dumplings.

This ragout may be made of capon, quail, hazel hen, snow hen, pheasant or snipe.

No. 43—BLACKBIRDS.

Quantity for 6 Persons.

12 blackbirds
¼ lb. of butter
1 pinch of salt
1 pinch of pepper
½ tbsp. of flour
½ tbsp. of white wine
½ cup of water or broth
6 juniper berries

For Stuffing.

The intestines of the birds
2½ rolls
½ tsp. of lemon juice

Some salt and pepper
2 tbsps. of butter

Preparation: The blackbirds must be fresh. They are cleaned, the head skinned, the eyes taken out and bill and claws chopped off a bit. The legs are turned inward, the right foot stuck through the eye sockets and the claws joined. The intestines are taken out and the gizzard removed. Juniper berries and the cleaned intestines are chopped fine, seasoned with salt, pepper, ½ teaspoonful of lemon juice and 2 tablespoonfuls of butter. This stuffing is put into the birds and the openings closed, fastening with toothpicks. They are then closely packed into a pan and the browned hot butter poured on, seasoned with more salt, pepper and 5 pulverized juniper berries, then fried 15 minutes, turning them over several times. The rolls are sliced and toasted, placed on a platter and the birds arranged neatly on the toast after removing the toothpicks. For the gravy, brown ½ tablespoonful of flour in the drippings, add water, wine, cook, strain and serve with the birds.

You may drip some gravy on the toasted roll slices to make them more palatable.

No. 44—LEIPZIG LARKS.

These birds are prepared just like the blackbirds in No. 43. The intestines may also be used for the filling.

No. 45—FRIED SNIPES.

Quantity for 6 Persons.

3 snipes
¼ lb. of butter
Salt, pepper
½ tbsp. of flour
1½ toasted rolls
Some broth

Bacon slices to tie around them

Preparation: The snipes are prepared the same as the blackbirds or larks in No. 43 and No. 44. The gizzard is removed, the bacon slices are tied around the birds, after salting and peppering inside and outside; then fry them in butter for 20 minutes and serve them on the toast which has been soaked with some of the gravy.

For the gravy, stir ½ tablespoonful of flour into the drippings, add broth, cook, strain and serve with the birds. These are garnished with snipe on toast made from the intestines.

No. 46—SNIPE ON TOAST.

Quantity for 6 Persons.

Intestines from the 3 birds with the gizzard removed
1½ tbsps. of butter
1 yolk of egg
1½ tbsps. of red wine
1 tsp. of chopped capers
Salt, pepper
A few drops of lemon juice
¼ cup of bread crumbs
2½ rolls, sliced
Some butter
1 tbsp. Parmesan cheese

Preparation: The cleaned intestines are chopped and mixed well with butter, yolk of egg, red wine, parsley, capers, salt, pepper, bread crumbs and lemon juice. Cut the rolls in slices ½ inch thick, cut off the crust, toast them and put the above stuffing on thick, sprinkle some Parmesan cheese over and drip melted butter on, then bake them in the oven for 5 minutes and place around the fried snipes.

No. 47—FRIED WOODCOCK.

Quantity for 6 Persons.

1 woodcock
¼ lb. of butter
⅛ lb. of bacon for larding
Salt
¾ qt. of sour cream
½ pt. of bouillon or broth

Preparation: The woodcock may hang 5 days before being cooked. Skin, dress and pound it, wash and dry it well and salt it inside and outside, then lard with bacon. The woodcock is fried in the butter, the cream and broth are poured on gradually and the bird stewed for 2 hours, basting frequently. By this time the gravy will be boiled down and smooth, strain it and serve with the bird.

No. 48—ANOTHER FORM OF FRIED WOODCOCK.

Quantity for 6 Persons.

1 woodcock or hen
1 bottle of red wine
1 bottle wine vinegar
3 bay-leaves
10 pepper-corns
7 cloves
1 onion, sliced
1 carrot, sliced
A little thyme
Bacon slices
⅛ lb. of butter
Salt
1 pt. sour cream
1 pt. bouillon

Preparation: The woodcock is cleaned, dressed, tied, pressed into a jar and the bottle of red wine is emptied into this. The vinegar is boiled together with bay-leaves, pepper-corns, cloves, onion, carrot, thyme and when cooled, also poured on the bird; in this it remains 2 to 3 days.

After this time the bird is taken out, dried, rubbed with salt, bacon slices tied around it, fried in the butter, and stewed for 2 hours, basting frequently with cream and bouillon. The gravy is strained, the bacon slices are taken off the bird. It is served on a platter, some gravy poured over the bird and the rest served separately.

Remarks: You may serve a Madeira or pickle gravy with it.

No. 49—ROAST WILD DUCK.

Quantity for 6–8 Persons.

2 young, wild ducks
1 pt. water
⅛ lb. of butter
Bacon slices
2 cloves
1 bay-leaf
1 onion, sliced
2 tbsps. of flour
1 wineglassful of red wine
Salt 6 pepper-corns

Preparation: The ducks are picked, singed, dressed, washed and skinned, salted inside and outside and tied into bacon slices. The prepared ducks are put into a stewpot over the fire with 1 pt. of water, onion, cloves, pepper-corns, bay-leaves. Cover and stew. When the water is boiled down, pour the ⅛ lb. of hot butter over them and add a little water or broth so that the butter may not get too brown, also add the red wine. 15 minutes before they are done, stir in the flour, add more broth or water if necessary and cook. The ducks should be of a nice golden brown color. Serve them with the strained gravy.

No. 50—ROAST CAPONS.

Quantity for 6 Persons.

1 capon
Salt
¼ lb. of butter
Bacon for larding

For the Gravy.

1 tbsp. of flour
1 tbsp. of wine

Preparation: The capon is picked, dressed, the breast and drum sticks larded with bacon, and the bird salted inside and outside. Then the hot butter is poured over it and roasted 1¼ hours until done, basting frequently with cream.

For the gravy, brown the flour in the drippings, add the wine, and broth or water, cook, strain and serve with the bird.

No. 51—FRIED CAPON RAGOUT.

May be made from the capon. Prepare it just the same as described in [No. 42](), Fine Partridge Ragout.

No. 52—STEWED CAPON.

Quantity for 6 Persons.

1 capon
Salt
6 pepper-corns
2 onions, sliced
⅛ of a celery

½ carrot, sliced
1 clove
1 wineglassful of red wine
1 tsp. of lemon juice
1 tsp. of sugar
½ pt. champignons
Some bouillon or water
⅛ lb. of butter
2 tbsps. of flour
1 bay-leaf

Preparation: The capon is prepared well and tied into bacon slices, then fried in ⅛ lb. butter for ½ hour.

For the gravy, stir in the flour, fill up with bouillon or water mixed with a teaspoonful of meat extract and the rest of the ingredients and in this gravy stew the capon 45 minutes to 1 hour, basting and turning it frequently. Serve the capon and strain the gravy. Quarter the champignons and put them into the gravy. Pour in the champignon juice while stewing.

Remarks: You can take oysters instead of champignons, allowing 3 or 4 to each person. Before serving the bird, remove bacon and strings.